Room no.1023 (un:

MW01673663

Writat publishers

Writat, Cowrks, Ground Floor, WorldMark-1, Aerocity, New Delhi 110037, India

Writat LLC, 312 W. 2nd St #1880 Casper, WY 82601, USA

Written by author Shreyas Ghadge

Edited by author Shreyas Ghadge

designed by Author Shreyas Ghadge

ROOM NO 1023

(Unsolved murder mystery)

Part 1

By Shreyas Ghadge

ABOUT THE AUTHOR

Shreyas Ghadge, a civil engineering student completed his engineering in 2022 from YCCE College of Engineering. But his writing journey started from childhood, he brought his interest in writing to this field at a very young age. And using very big words, he has framed every subject according to himself. For which he has also been honored with various awards. Author Shreyas Ghadge has given many hundreds of thoughts on human nature to the people through the book. In fact, even those experiences for which it is a matter of great experience, he has published through the word in an excellent amount through books and his articles. Not only this, but his belief is that a person should look at his passion at least once, along with the fact that civil engineering is his profession and writing is his passion, even though these two things are different, their importance is the same in his life.

ABOUT THE NOVEL

First of all, this novel is based on a true incident. The secret that most people still don't know. A murder in a hotel room number 1023 reveals some very hidden secrets, but until the end it is not known who committed the murder. Even after a thorough investigation, small and large cases related to it are solved. But till the end it is not known that any person came in that room who committed the murder but no one in that room Someone is seen coming and not leaving, so how did he get killed? Was it a suicide case? What spirit was in that room? There are many secrets that many people will know after reading but cannot be told through words. The last part which is presented is purely imaginary. But it is logical to think that such things can happen. And after reading the complete novel somewhere one can claim that maybe there will be a second part too. The entire incident may be shown in the second part as well

Index

"Sir sir come quickly.........look what happened here".... screamed the hotel maid Meera. In no time, a crowd was formed. From the hotel manager to the entire hotel staff......... And in no time the entire people were literally scared to death. Looking at the picture in front of them, it was as if the ground beneath each person's feet disappeared. It was a sight so hideous and horrible that every one's state would be seized from every particle of the heart after seeing it. At that time, one of the activists said in his scared voice with courage. "Call the police immediately and ask them to come as soon as possible..." The hotel manager ordered the entire crowd to wait for them in the hotel hall until the police arrived. The police staff immediately took him to that room 1023 and immediately DCP Raghav's eyes were filled with surprise. Because I had seen so many murders before this, but the scene of the picture that I faced was the same even after closing my eyes was being imprinted in the brain. And here begins the story of a mysterious murder in room number 1023.

Chapter 1- The earliest recognition of this complete nuisance

DCP Raghav in conversation with Sub

Inspector Ashish says after a mention of the whole thing above "Ashish didn't you feel scared for your life for the first time seeing this? I mean for you murder cases are no big deal and no surprise." But in all these years of service, no one has seen such a dangerous victim, so I asked "... On that Sub Inspector Ashish said "Yes Sir. In fact, I don't know which horse was killed for murder so that he got such a terrible reward. The other person gave it in the form of murder."

Then DCP Raghav says, send to meet the manager of this hotel. DCP Raghav asked the manager

"How many years have you been the manager of this hotel?"

Manager says "Sir last 7 years". On that DCP Raghav says "It's surprising that in seven years you may have heard the news of murders but never guessed that your experience of all these years has come across these things." Actually, I am not doubting your professional life. But you It is a little curious that there was no anticipation of any kind of forewarning of the murder." To which the manager nervously replies "Sorry sir but in my years of service I have never suspected any person like that. Because we have treated every person well every time in our hotel, we have never looked at them from that point of view." DCP Raghav "Whoever saw this murder first, call her" Maid Meera tells the whole truth to DCP Raghav sir. "Sir, I was the first to see him in this condition." But I didn't know what to do, so I called the manager." DCP Raghav gets emotional and says

"Look I can understand all these things are very difficult for you to deal with." But the job of the police is to keep a close eye on everything, so you remember the person who came in, who disappeared in the room, or who you suspect to be the murderer of this person. Have already stayed at this hotel to not?" Then Meera, the maid, answers with fear. "Sir, I am a very poor housewife, I don't have much time to pay attention to anyone. My job is just cleaning the hotel and delivering the stuff to all the rooms in the hotel. So, I really have no idea what person can come and go in the room. "

DCP Raghav says to manager "Well, well, let's talk about this later… First of all, you should give me the complete details of the person who was murdered, that is, his residence, how long he has been here, his full name, what he does, why he came here, etc. Will send it to the police station by Sub Inspector Ashish's hand." And then calling DCP Raghav Ashish "body foreign sick lab sent all the photos of this complete room on my desk in file form till evening. Keep." By then I also question the hotel owner. On that Sub Inspector Ashish "Yes sir the forensic team has been informed and collection of all the blood samples from the room has also started. When the owner of the hotel, meets DCP Raghav, without asking anything, he begins to reveal his secrets to him. Hotel owner Mishra ji "Sir sure there is a plan to defame my hotel so that our hotel will be seen in a bad light. The man who was killed in our hotel We don't even know him who has died." DCP Raghav laughs at that and says "What happened Mishraji. Just like every criminal repeats the poem that I did not kill you are repeating the same film dialogue in front of us. Now the world has changed so much that it is important that the media knows everything before the police. It has happened because their network and the public trust them more than the police because if there is any murder tomorrow, the media will help them."

"Oh no no sir you are taking my fancy the wrong way." Said the hotel owner. I didn't mean that, because for a long time our hotel started receiving such threats. Our hotel has made great progress in a very short time. Because of which these things became visible in the eyes of the whole people." So perhaps we are suspected of doing such things to defame our hotel.'" DCP Raghav then says, "Look, Mishraji, I am comparing your professional world with this murder case. Not doing Because your preaching has nothing to do with this murder in my opinion. If at that moment you met the same person in the state in which he was found there, you did not in any way hint that they had anything to do with your infamy." "Yes sir, but most of the time in such cases every policeman's suspicion always falls on the hotel owner." Mishraji says to DCP Raghav sir. On that, DCP Raghav says, "You seem to be watching movies too much Which makes you feel like you have a lot of experience in such things". Anyways, if we need any help from you, we will contact you. Also, whenever you are called by the police station, you will have to come, and along with this, you should not go outside the city without taking the permission of the police, permission will be given only if there is some very important work," said DCP Raghav. From there they directly reach the police station. Sub Inspector Ashish after meeting DCP Raghav tells him the whole truth "Sir this case There are things related to her that will surprise even the person who suffered from it." DCP Raghav asks, "Why, what happened, we had many such cases, but still, we did not solve them……. then what new things were found in these cases??" Sub Inspector Ashish "Sir I inquired with the hotel staff.... this person was staying in their hotel for three days was strange…. I mean sir it would be bad to talk about any person but really the person's habits, behavior, movement and not only that but also his appearance, he came to that hotel in a very bad shape." That makes it a bit difficult to say what type of person he was." On that DCP Raghav says "Well well… all these things are a bit personal; we cannot judge someone's profession and intelligence from his living. As I said related to this case. If you bring as much information as you have to my table, will you do it?" Sir wanted to say that no document related to that person properly could be found. So, there was no point in creating a partial file. So, we find it a bit difficult to start the case except once we have to talk to the manager and his daughter Meera in some detail. Then after next day the police visited the hotel again when they heard many such facts.

Chapter 2 Interrogation of DCP Raghav along with Hotel Staff

Then the next day when they reach the hotel

with the police staff, the manager DCP Raghav says, "Excuse me sir, but yesterday Mishra sir told us to inform you that the police should not enter directly. Sub-inspector Ashish said, "Why is that so?" The hotel manager says, "Actually sir, the rest of the people staying in the hotel are very scared. You come here in that condition, so the repetition of the hotel and the attitude of the people is going through a little different way.is." DCP Raghav laughs and says, "Well, now we should take your permission and do the work of the government. Look, we are doing our work and keep in mind that there has been a murder, so every person will question our coming and going here. Suspiciousness is going to happen at the top so we're doing our job and you're doing yours. And there are lodges and orders that we have to follow as well." There is no simple murder. If such things happen in our life Think about it as you have seen the events related to it, and if there is someone from your house tomorrow, think about it in that spirit." The manager says “Sorry sir. Then sub-inspector Ashish says "As many servants and maids as you have in your hotel staff, call them soon." DCP Raghav then confronts the maid Meera before questioning everyone. And says "Look Meera you might think our questions are a bit stilted but our job is That’s one guess to make, and you were the one who saw the corpse first." To which Meera says "Yes sir. I can understand." DCP Raghav says to the manager "How do you inform your hotel of a new arrival who is going to stay here". On that the manager says "Actually sir we take all the things under legal process. But now it's vacation time so many staff members are on vacation.... he too because the hotel rates are high these days. And we were doing the procedure as quickly as possible." DCP Raghav on this says "All these things are fine but the identity proof of the person who has been living here for three days will be asked". The manager says "yes sir but what happened was that it was raining heavily and when he came to the hotel his whole body was wet so the ID could not be scanned." "Well call the employee who made his entry." Ordered by DCP Raghav gave Kishore from staff came... Kishore said "Yesterday sir I also told sub inspector Ashish sir everything about him." On that Sub Inspector Ashish says "Yes sir I took this same statement yesterday." DCP Raghav says "Okay, what name did he tell us at the reception?" Alok Purohit, he made his entry under this name." “Would you tell me briefly about him now that he was wet but what did you think about him?” asked DCP Raghav sir. On that Kishore says "Sir the seemed to me a very strange man. Actually, he doesn't deserve to come to such a good hotel.... because before coming to such a good hotel a person should have some manners. But from his behavior and the toning of his speech, the person did not seem very educated. And there was a cut above his eye. And there was no standard in speaking. That is, he certainly did not seem to be a man of some great post." After hearing this statement DCP Raghav gave a smile to Kishore He is asked "Mr. Kishor Proper where are you from?" On that, Kishore shyly tells the name of his village. And then DCP Raghav says "then we can say the same Kishore that you also don't deserve to stand in this hotel? If you are talking down to people, how do you treat yourself as a human being?" Kishore then says "sorry sir I shouldn't say this but I found that person's behavior really strange and I was avoiding him as if he doesn't want to stay in this hotel because there is a lot of workloads in ready vacation." But even after we refused them repeatedly, they decided to stay in Room One Zero Two Three. We also thought that if we tell the price of this room, it might refuse and walk away bored. But instead of doing that, he decided to stay here. And paid the money in full in one stroke." "Well, once you read what they mentioned in your information Why?" DCP Raghav asked. On that Kishore says "Actually, the rain was coming through so much that his document was wet. So, I took down the things he said in the register. He didn't say much. Name Alok Purohit. Age 37 years, proper Raipur and given phone number sir." DCP Raghav asks "When he came to the hotel, did anyone else come with him or was he alone?" No sir he came alone no one was with him Not only that, but he had brought with him only a small bag containing a book and a pen for signing. Apart from this, I could find nothing." Did they say anything about their profession like what they were doing or what field they were working in? Kishore replies, "No sir, they have not mentioned anything in the register. Not only that, but when I was writing in the register, they said that I will write the name in my own letters." And When DCP Raghav looks at the register, there is the person's handwriting in very fine letters, his signature looks so professional as if a film star of a big movie gives his autograph. From all the information so far, DCP Raghav felt that this person is not a simple person at all. TCP Raghav's mind was saying somewhere that this person has some connection with some big organization. And according to what the whole staff mentions and observes think this person has the complete opposite view of what he is expressing. Sub Inspector Ashish asks DCP Raghav. "Sir what do you think from the information you have received so far this person is from some big area or just a commoner who was accidentally killed?" DCP Raghav says "Look Ashish we are not looking at something big from the right angle. As easy as we think this case is, it could be very wrong." Somewhere I feel that someone who belongs to someone There seems to be a possibility of connection with a larger field and organization. You see, I don't think the signature that this person has made is probably not his, and the pen with which his name is written is also expensive in the market. This is the mistake people make by identifying a person by his clothes and shoes but not considering what the real value of that person is based on his letters and his writing style." At that time, a policeman from the police staff called "Sir Forensic from Fonzo, you have been called to see me." Further, after going to the forensic lab, some similar things were seen in depth

Chapter 3 Forensic report received by DCP Raghav

After reaching the forensics, Dr. Kritika lays out the whole story to DCP Raghav and presents one point at a time. Doctor Kritika "Good afternoon, Raghav sir...Actually we wanted to make a report but before making the report, we called you as it is important for you to complete everything in the form." DCP Raghav says "yes yes if you did it right then tell me what will be your conclusion." Doctor Kritika "Yes sir, actually sir the victim was hit with more than ten stab wounds. But however, it is very difficult to tell if he was killed or if he did it on his own. Because it is natural that in such a beating, the blood of the murderer should also come out. But we did not find any other blood marks on the victim. Another suspicious thing is that Vicky was not under the influence of any kind of alcohol, but it is natural that he screamed while murdering or was beaten so much, so once you have to do an on-the-spot investigation." Maximum age of persons is 40 to 4Must be in the 5-age range. It is evident that the person was very much in the habit of smoking and also it was more than eight hours after the murder and the body was declared to have been found three hours late." Thinking about it, DCP Raghav says, "What could be the reason for giving it three hours late, Ashish?" She Ashish says, "Sir, the staff or the owner may have something to do with this." And DCP Raghav says "Just the staff and who else are we missing?" I mean sir who else is “it related to the case?" DCP Raghav asks Kritika "Doctor, did you find anything else because we can put some emphasis on your statement so far the statements heard are different and when we closely observe them, they come out different so in such condition we will focus more on your words." Kritika laughs at that and says, "Also, sir, we have not found anything special, but we have seen only so many things in the analysis we have done so far."The victim has been stabbed with a knife or some sharp object and no marks of wear and tear have been found on the body. Another stab wound was found at the back of the neck with a tool, probably from the hands of some mailman." Hearing this, DCP Raghav got a little worried. And thinking about it, they started talking to each other about it, "Ashish, what do you think we should draw from Kritika's statement?" On that Ashish says "Sir I like this think it is more likely to be a suicide case than a murder, because as you can see, Alok Purohit came to stay in this hotel and his behavior was a little strange compared to other people. When we look at the whole thing in that room from above, it looks like a very gruesome murder, and sir how is it possible that such a gruesome murder took place but the neighbors of the room didn't even know about it." "Then let's meet the room neighbors too" says DCP Raghav. Then in the hotel After leaving, DCP Raghav says "We want the key of the murdered room and meet the people living around the room." The family living next door came from Delhi. (Pandey Family) DCP Raghav says "Hello I am DCP Raghav, sorry sir we disturbed you but it is very important to communicate with you related to a case. So, we are here." Then Mr. Pandey from Pandey family speaks "hello sir, actually four days leave from office so I am going to my Came here for a walk with my family, I really don't know who committed the murder in the neighboring room, infect I have never seen that person before". But my wife and my son were telling me that he was a very strange man indeed. Not only was his attitude very frightening, but he was also very ugly in appearance, which is what we feared the most." DCP Raghav says "well, you were left to admire the person.... that's what he looks like., ugly, whatever.......... This is not your issue. All I want to hear is where were you yesterday when they were murdered." Then Mr. Pandey says "Sir we are in this room since yesterday because our tour got shifted to the next day so we were here all day to do it but we didn't hear any kind of screaming or things breaking etc." DCP Raghav says "How do you know what kind of things are noise in their room came?" To which Mr. Pandey nervously replies "No sir we thought you were asking something like that so I replied that I didn't feel any movement in the next room wrong..." On that DCP Raghav again smiles and replies, "That's great, before the questions, your answers are ready, first Mishraji and now you...." Mr. Pandey says "yes nothing like that sir actually me and friend are childhood friends so I always come to hotel. and whenever I When he comes, he prefers to stay in room number one zero to four." After hearing this DCP Raghav laughs and says "You are not childhood friends but childhood brothers...one should learn to answer questions from you anyways like I warned them I warn you too until we get any lead related to this case you Arun number one zero Relax in Two Four and don't go back to Delhi without informing the police and tell them that the tour has been extended a bit ok. Have a nice day." Inspector Ashish "Sir do you think Mr. Pandey and his family have anything to do with this murder?" DCP Raghav "How come we can't say anything right now but we don't understand something, why does everyone think this person's behavior is better than others?" Another thing is if this person is between 40 to 45 i.e., 37 as he mentions then he should be married. with which family he came and for what reason he came is still unknown. It's not." At that time, Inspector Ashish says, "We have arranged a schedule to invite the family for body verification by three o'clock today. So, we will try to contact their family today, sir." Once from the manager and from the forensic team, Alok Purohit tried to contact him by confiscating all the materials he had brought with him and also his phone number. Tomorrow we will search the room properly. And after that, when the next day the entire scenario takes the case through a different path when the room is searched.

Chapter 4 Room search conducted by DCP Raghav

DCP Raghav and his police force attended room number one zero two three along with their entire contents for thorough investigation. Looking at the room closely, DCP Raghav closes his eyes and tries to imagine the whole thing once. Then DCP Raghav asked sub-inspector Ashish, "Ashish, what exactly happened before the murder in this room?" Ashish replied, "Sir, I think Mr. Purohit must have been murdered by someone who knew him. Because the way our investigation has been conducted so far, it is possible that the person entering the room would have known Mr. Purohit." DCP Raghav said, "But if we think from a different angle, it could also be that someone is already present in the room. Or it could also be that someone who keeps coming into the room can be behind it. Because the most important point in killing any person is Means "time". Any work due to lack of time cannot be successful. For the discernment of what time the other person works and what time he rests further helps the murderer." On this Sub Inspector Ashish says "But sir this is also surprising how the murderer managed to escape from this room in such a short time? That too when there is CCTV footage all over this hotel. We also checked the footage yesterday but no one. In such footage, someone was seen entering the room and if not, someone was seen walking into the room." DCP Raghav said, "How is it that any murderer commits some kind of mistake, or it may be that we have to look at the case from a slightly different angle, like if the intruder is an acquaintance of theirs or a relative of theirs?" It could be any person staying in the hotel, a person who may be familiar with the corners of this hotel.

Therefore, it is not wrong to look at any person with suspicion., the telling people at Karki Hotel and my point of view don't quite match." On that Sub Inspector Ashish said "I don't understand anything sir." DCP Raghav says "Oh look, everyone was saying the same thing that Mr. Purohit's behavior was very strange, but look, even after the murder in this room, everything is kept in its proper place. Now if the murderer doesn't have so much time. That he would put everything in place, Mr. Purohit That would be it, one more thing from everyone's story that they wanted to say that Mr. Former seemed to be a very village and unbranded person. Just look at the cigarette that is lying on the side maybe Mr. was already using it and there are very few people who can afford it. Look at that person's pen, look at the letters, from what angle do you think this person is an uneducated person and comes from a small village? At that time, an inspector said, "Sir, come to the bathroom quickly and see what you see here?" DCP Raghav and Sub Inspector When Ashish goes to the bathroom, he finds that Mr. Purohit had been heavily scuffled before he was killed, as signs of wear and tear are visible not in the room but in the bathroom. DCP Raghav tells Sub Inspector Ashish "It looks like someone hit their head on it forcefully. That's why we see such a big bend here." Sub Inspector Ashish "But sir these things are not mentioned in the forensic report so maybe this bend belongs to the person who did the murder too. Could be." At that DCP Raghav smiles and says "Smart Ashish, you have developed the art of observing things closely in a very short time." And just then, less than a meter away, she meets an earring under the window. DCP Raghav says as soon as he takes the earring in his hands "Now the history of this earring will be told only by Meera madam from the hotel staff". "What are you saying sir?" asked Sub Inspector Ashish. DCP Raghav says "Yes, why don't you like to hear parables? Just like that one parable is going to be heard". DCP Raghav said to another inspector, "See what I am telling you, complete the instructions by tomorrow and give me an update soon." First of all, the desired information about this person has not yet reached us like his family, what the person was doing, and also his background. So, contact the hotel staff and collect information by circulating a proper sketch or photo of it throughout the place. And help get this out in the media." Till then me and Sub Inspector Ashish Go to Meera Madam and hear a parable about how her jhumka came to the window."

Chapter 5 A personal conversation related to the case of maid Meera

As soon as he reaches the hotel, DCP Raghav

says "I want to question the manager Miss Meera again so call her once to give her statement." Manager "yes sir one minute.... Then while Sub Inspector Ashish and DCP Raghav are sitting in the rest room, maid Meera comes there. And before any questioning, they directly ask her the question "Why did you kill Mr. Purohit?" After hearing this sentence, Sub Inspector Ashish and other employees are completely surprised. That surprise the important reason behind it was DCP Raghav's voice and his confidence too.......m Meera said, "What are you talking about, sir? I don't know anything." (Very scared DCP Raghav then says "Look we don't have much time so confess your crime. And surrender soon. On the day of the murder, you saw the deadest body, and we found your earring there as evidence. Then Inspector Ashish tells DCP Raghav. "Sir, this jhumka belongs to Meera from what? These days fashion is growing in a big way Ashish you wouldn't know I can claim this jhumka belonged to Meera. When we saw Meera on the day of the murder... an earring was missing from her ear. And not only that, seeing her fashion sense, the color of the watch always matches her earrings. Even today, look at the color of her hair and the jhumka in her ear." said DCP Raghav To which Meera said "Sir this story is true...that jhumka is mine but I Mr. purohit killed him did not "Mira madam every murderer gives the same answer before asking the question so I allowed you to confess directly" said DCP Raghav. "Sir I am telling you why I would kill them if I didn't even know them properly," Mira said "Even if you don't know them, how did you find your jhumka under the window? That too, from the door of room no. 1023." On that Meera starts crying... and while crying she says "Sir believe me I am real “I did not kill them. I admit that my jhumka fell there, but I have nothing to do with their murder." On that the lady officer slaps Meera twice and says "Why are you doing emotional blackmail by crying like this, does anyone here have no feelings, come to the police station, when the punishment falls on our hands, your mouth will come out right away." DCP Raghav then tells the lady officer to stop and very respectfully once again asks Meera "Look Meera tell us whatever you know otherwise we will have There are many ways to find answers to questions that may trouble you." Meera thinks about it and slowly gives her opinion "Sir first day when Mr. Purohit came to the hotel, he was very wet due to rain. And it is my duty to provide proper service in the room. Sub Inspector Ashish then asks, "Well then what happened next that you didn't tell us on the day of the murder, but we asked you on that day too. Then you told all these things. No, what actually happened." "That day sir I was very scared because I saw such a horrible murder for the first time in my literal life and I was speechless when I saw the police coming. And the manager sir also warned us not to let anything go out." On that DCP Raghav looks at the manager in anger.... then the manager says scared "Sir we were given an order by Mishra sir so that the hotel should not be defamed so we staff These things were told in "Mira tell me what happened next I also see who is defaming whom and who is the killer" said DCP Raghav. Meera continues, "I took Mr. Purohit to the room. Actually sir, he seemed to be a bit of an introvert. He didn't like to talk to anyone much. Even in the elevator, he was standing far away from me. And as soon as I reached the room, I thanked him. asked to go." Meera further says "Then the next day when I cleaned the room When He came to do it, he looked very pensive as if he was thinking about something. And while cleaning he suddenly asked me a question "How long have you been working here?" Meera "Sir I am from last three years". Mr. Purohit "Father, what education did you have?" "Sir I am a graduate but there is no earner at home so I have to do part time work" Mira said. "Oh my God, even with education, the situation brings a person into conflict somewhere," said Mr. Purohit. On its Meera says yes sir but work has to be done, what shame of work... Mr. Purohit says "very nice son surely you will be successful one day". DCP Raghav said, "You have succeeded Mr. Purohit by murdering him..." Further Meera says "We used to have this conversation every day. the time it took to clean the room was the only time we used to talk because their cigarettes also lasted that long." DCP Raghav says "Wow very good did you hear Ashish. Till yesterday the person whose behavior It seems strange that today when you ask him deeply, he suddenly becomes humble." She also laughs at that. And smilingly says "Raghav sir you are really an Antaramian you knew you were going to hear a parable." Meera repeats the same sentence over and over "Sir indeed I have not killed Mr. Purohit. And no, I have anything to do with him." DCP Raghav says "Meera madam I asked you a question how did you find your jhumka there….and here you meet you and Mr. Purohit. You're telling the truth." Meera says, "Sir, the next day when I went to change the towels, the whole room was dusty and the whole room was dark at 7:30 PM. Mr. Purohit didn't have any light on it. So, I was very scared." Meera further says, "His voice suddenly changed and he was talking and saying I like to stay like this and leave with a towel." For a while everyone will be in a suspicious mind listens to And DCP Raghav gets a bit suspicious. And in a suspicious mood they ask Meera "Mira tell me for sure was its Mr. Purohit or someone else? Because he found his dead body the very next day." To which Meera says "Sir the voice was different but as far as I could see he was

Mr. Purohit. And the cigarette he used to smoke was the same smell." DCP Raghav thought for a while he was thrusting his head wondering what kind of prospect there was once even his eyes. He closed his eyes and tried to recreate the scene in his imagination. Then they came up with a trick. And DCP Raghav says to Meera, "Okay, Meera, put your signature on this statement and I will take care of the rest." While signing, DCP Raghav looked at the receipt very closely. And left the hotel without taking that statement. Then sub-inspector Ashish goes behind DCP Raghav in surprise and comes out of the hotel. An ask "Sir what did you do? You asked her to give the statement and while signing, he came back without taking the paper." DCP Raghav says "No Ashish she is nobody." Sub Inspector Ashish asks "Sir when you confessed your crime to her in front of everyone, I felt you were very confident and I also felt that the case was solved immediately. And now you are saying she is nobody." On that DCP

Raghav says "I have read Ashish Forewing's report sir Someone who killed Purohit is a left hander. And while signing Mira, I looked closely for it because she is a right hander. "But sir then how did that jhumka come there?" asked Sub Inspector Ashish "Actually, I'm dealing with a clue related to the case, not someone's personal life." DCP Raghav said. At that Ashish is completely surprised and asks "So sir I don't know anything." DCP Raghav says, "Look, Ashish, Inspector, you are doing your duty, but this thing is too much. It is true that there are many things which if not faced, one's life will run smoothly. As much as I think so. Mr. Purohit was a bit of a sex addict... so the maid might have taken advantage of Meera by taking him to the window and trying to force her and her jhumka fell there in the process." Sub Inspector Ashish asks "But sir how can you say this with so much confidence!!!" DCP Raghav says "So much experience so far will not lie.... Meera continues her It was not that she was trying to hide her neck scar, but she felt that if she made this statement, she might lose her job, so she was continuously hiding her neck scar and told everything while telling but she was avoiding somewhere while telling the story. And I tried to put an end to that because if the lady inspector had hit her again in one fell swoop, she might have had to be humiliated in front of everyone. Which I didn't approve of at all. getting sad As Ashish often suffers injustice, women behave like this." As soon as Meera hears this conversation between DCP Raghav and Sub Inspector Ashish, a different basis is formed in her mind towards DCP Raghav and she prays to God and says, "Finally God has sent someone to listen to my prayers." Then DCP Raghav says "Come on Ashish take the car to the police station." When Meera and DCP Raghav catch sight of each other, Meera bows to them. And DCP Raghav leaves with a smile.

Chapter 6 Complete information so far given to Commissioner Sir.

Sub Inspector Ashish "Raghav sir seriously I am very lucky that I got to work under you in fact till now I have worked with many senior officers. But in the rush to close the case they never knew the feelings of a person. But you are not like that. You judge the other person by maturity as well." DCP Raghav and his entire team reach the police station with a smile on that. After reaching the police station…. Constable "Sir just now Commissioner sir the call came and they called you to the office and were a little angry, so if you spoke in anger ask them to bring the file too..." On that DCP Raghav says to Inspector Ashish "Come on Ashish now we have been called to tell the parable. I don't know how many hours Commissioner Sir will have to do the conveyance today." Sub Inspector Ashish and DCP Raghav arrive at Commission Sir's office with complete documents related to the case. Then commissioner sir "come in.... what update so far..." DCP Raghav says “Sir, stay in the case Such a lead has not been met yet. Our investigation is going on but a lot of things are coming to light in the investigation so it is difficult to make any decision." Commissioner Sir "Look Raghav, I have full faith in you and you will solve this case soon. But solve this case as soon as possible...Already I am very tense with the media. Also, as I told you that the promotion has, I have a slightly different focus. So, it shouldn't go." DCP Raghav says yes sir I remember everything but the case is really a bit critical." Tell me what happened from the beginning... Sub Inspector Ashish opens the full file and says, "Sir, on September 14, a person came to stay in the hotel as Mr. Alok Purohit for three days. After arriving, he did not find any material, only a book, an expensive pen, and cigarettes. At most, if the majority were to be seen, all people would find his behavior extremely strange and a strange mark would be placed on his head. It was It is also difficult to say what was his exact profession as everyone said. And even when there was an improper document, he was given a look." Commissioner sir asks "Is there any reason behind this because maximum hotel doesn't do document less entry!!!" "Yes, sir the room given to him was very expensive room number one zero two three. Another thing to wonder is that people who know that hotel never stayed in that room for some special reason. It didn't fall." Ashish said. Commissioner Sir says "Well then what happens next?" On that DCP Raghav said, "Sir, we started investigating in that room and started questioning all the people. For questioning, everyone's statement was changing as per what was said, so it is a bit difficult to say what is true 100%. CCTV footage was also seen and no person was seen coming at the time of the murder. After the murder, when he was leaving. According to the forensic report, if there is any information No such drugs have been given. There were so many stab wounds on the body but there is no suspicion of another person's blood. Also, the only lead we have in the current situation is that the murderer is mostly left-handed." "Which person is more suspicious?" Commissioner sir asked DCP Raghav says "Sir it's a bit difficult because in the present situation no one can be trusted and no one's statement can make much sense. “Is." "Look try to finish this case as soon as possible in the next ten days because the media is getting a bit difficult to handle. Not only that, but also put pressure on the suspect to confess and release him as soon as possible. If you need any help, let me know. Permits from here. You may come now." While coming out of the cabin, Sub Inspector Ashish tells DCP Raghav, "Commissioner sir, I feel stranger than a murdered person." DCP Raghav says with a smile "Now when the greed of promotion is released in such a big way, any person will do the same in greed. Everyone is looking for their own benefit. Ashish who wants to increase his TRP through media, who wants to take promotion. And we have a parable of this, and it does not suggest an early ending. So, what came has to be written down." On that Ashish says "You are right sir, but why am I still suspicious of Meera. because she is the one sir who has a strong motive to kill Mr. Purohit. "So, we should look into this once sir." DCP Raghav says "No Ashish, it's not easy for a maid to commit such a big murder. Such people are too afraid of their image. They care a lot if someone sees them as a criminal, so they suffer injustice but dare to raise voice against it. Neither does. Now it's hard to say whether that's the right thing or the wrong thing." Just then Sub Inspector Ashish gets a call and he is the only one on the phone They lose their senses and a person on the phone says to them, "Sir, do something with this media. They are spreading wrong news. These people are telecasting news by giving wrong names to people. The real name of the person Alok Purohit is calling is Kailas Tripathi." DCP Raghav and Sub Inspector Ashish get stunned on hearing this sentence. And then they got the person's phone call to meet him directly and from here we get to hear a different history of Alok Purohit.

Chapter 7 Who was Kailas Tripathi?

Whoever you are talking to is at the police station immediately. After reaching the police station the person talking on the phone introduces himself "Sir I am professor in Sanjay Tiwari B.Sc. College Raipur, the person whose photo is given in the media whose poster I saw when I reached here is not Alok Purohit. The sketch is not recognizable. But his by looking at that mark on his head, I can say for sure that this is Professor Kailas Tripathi of our college." The entire police staff was stunned after hearing this sentence happen DCP Raghav then asks "How can you say this? Just look at this photo closely and then tell me." In fact, even before this was verified 100 percent, DCP Raghav felt somewhere in his heart that the person who had been murdered must be very intelligent and good. To this Sanjay Tiwari says "Sir we are in service since 2003 Kailas Tripathi is the only professor with PhD and also got many titles as a very intelligent scientist. But his behavior was changing day by day and some of his bad habits were declaring him a career hazard." Sub-inspector Ashish says, "Now smoking cigarettes is a strange and wrong habit, everyone does it." She says to Sanjay Tiwari, "Sir, cigarette pin was not his only habit, he had many other bad habits which were more dangerous than smoking cigarettes. He was a sex addict. Register your name in the racket. Due to which his wife also left him. And because of his voice, a woman even fell in love with him. Due to which he was also in jail for two years. But he also tried to fulfill his wish with the Chinese prisoner which caused him to be shifted from there to another prison. But being an intelligent scientist and also a renowned professor, he was released early but still many people suffer from it. He was also suspended from the college. He underwent many treatments but still did not improve. Finally, he got fed up and resigned from the research post and left Raipur but after that he never had any address. Today I was watching the same news and suddenly he appeared. Says sir that this is Kailas Tripathi." DCP Raghav and Sub Inspector Ashish was thinking He also didn't know what kind of comment is appropriate on this whole incident. And also, it is an important question why he registered his name as Alok Purohit in the hotel room number 1023. Then Sanjay Tiwari says "Sir Coincidence That I also have a photo of us from seven years ago at a college gathering. There may be a slight age difference then, but you can see the photo." After seeing the photo, he somewhere Sanjay Tiwari He believed in things. Along with Sanjay Tiwari, a sense of maturity also arose in his mind that if a professor is coming this far, then there must be a sense of understanding. Then DCP Raghav asks Sanjay Tiwari "Sanjay do you know any person as Alok Purohit?" Sanjay Tiwari says "No sir I myself wonder why Tripathi sir told his name Alok Purohit? Impact sir even any professor in our college, our friend There is no one as Alok Purohit." "Well thank you so much for coming this far and clearing the misunderstanding Alok Purohit had," said Sub Inspector Ashish. But DCP Raghav was still thinking. And after a few moments "Ok Tiwari sir you write your statement and sign here we have to add it to the document." Then seeing the pen drawn by Tiwari sir and writing with his left hand, DCP Raghav's needle of suspicion turned towards Tiwari sir. Let's see DCP Raghav's gesture After seeing the gesture, the eyes of the sub-inspector also turn to Tiwari sir, who is signing the signature. While keeping the pen, the same packet of cigarettes falls into the pocket of Tiwari Sir, the same brand which was seen by the murdered Kailash Tripathi. Professor Sanjay Tripathi came to tell the history but both the officers felt that a different history of theirs was hidden somewhere in this history. DCP Raghav "Tiwari sir how long have you been here? I mean it's not enough to come in one day, is it? Asked. Sanjay Tiwari says, "I always come here because most of our professors transferred here, so we have meetings." However, DCP Raghav respectfully says to him, "There are many things related to this case that can be done with your help while staying here for a few days." Sanjay Tiwari says "Yes, if you need any help, call me, I will come to the police station, now I am leaving, I want to meet some of my employees." Sub Inspector Ashish says "What a blessing, are you thinking the same thing I am?" "Yes, sir but no concrete proof just a guess. "Ashish says on that DCP Raghav says "Then why are you wasting your time, friend, activate your intelligence and order them to follow Tiwari sir to get internal marks. Let's see what kind of professor's staff and professor's contact are there."

Chapter 8 Tiwari's screen hangs

Sanjay Tiwari's visit may have been a treat for DCP Raghav and Sub Inspector Ashish. The suspicion of both of them was greatly increased. But taking Sanjay Tiwari into direct custody based on the information found in the investigation so far was impossible. Because any case always depends on the evidence. Therefore, no evidence about Sanjay Tiwari was present in the police station. Therefore, DCP Raghav could see only one way in all these developments. DCP Raghav says "I want a team of three officers to monitor only Sanjay Tiwari, where he goes, what he does, whether there is any taluka related to any criminal case in his past, collect information and present it to me in the next two installments..." So, everyone decided to do their job well and in a very short time they succeeded in gathering complete information about Sanjay Tiwari. The whole thing gives a new experience, when we meet a new person, we can never guess his past and his movements from his speech and behavior. The police came to know about Professor Sanjay Tiwari's many black dealings due to being under surveillance in the last two days. Along with that, the police also recorded Sanjay Tiwari's phone calls and observed through which number people used to call his number and on which number he used to talk the most. And further in this observation Many screens of Sanjay Tiwari had to be lifted by the police. Sub-Inspector Ashish informs DCP Raghav that "Sir in the whole investigation now Sanjay Tiwari has come to know about many reasons but I think he should be questioned once again." DCP Raghav "Yes yes of course my Sanjay grew on him by his two moves. In fact, the professor said that a different neck is created in the mind but only after seeing this he wanted to hit his neck with two jabs." SB Inspector Ashish says "But sir on this small suspicion will it be right to involve him in this case?" DCP Raghav laughs and says "You don't learn to swim until you jump into the water. So, let's drag Sanjay Tiwari into that water and see how much time Khari can spend in the water." The next day, Sanjay talks to Tiwari at the police station. Sanjay Tiwari asks without asking, "Oh, you needed me so much in my two-day visit, I didn't know I was so busy. “Is a person." On that DCP Raghav says "You are a working person; you only talk with Mr. David..." She said to Sanjay Tiwari, "What are you talking about sir? I have never even met anyone named David." DCP Raghav "Look professor sir we are not your students you will make us fool any theorem explain in your words and we will understand?" Many such people taught us theorem but we have made our own laws. SB Inspector Ashish says "Sanjay Tiwari tell me quickly what is your black business? And why did you commit the murder of Kailas Tripathi in this business?" Sanjay Tiwari is speechless and doesn't know what to say DCP Raghav says "What happened professor sir did you forget the lecture today? We have many methods which can tell you the answers very well". "Sir I really have no idea which David you are talking about," said Sanjay Tiwari. Sub Inspector Ashish says “Hey Look at the CCTV footage it's the same place the person you're talking to is David who supplies the drugs. And the continuous two hours your daily talked on the phone that your call record." And "By the way your CCTV footage was also seen in Kailash Tripathi's room," said DCP Raghav. This sentence of TCP Raghav put Sub Inspector Ashish and the entire police staff in a very big question? But surely this thing said by DCP Raghav may be useful to solve this case Everyone kept their expressions very serious thinking that this would happen. Sanjay Tiwari finally admitted "I'm sorry sir, I admit that I always took help from David to supply my drugs. And not only that, we also run a sex racket in which we also get funding from foreigners." Further Sanjay Tiwari says "For this we always send Kailash Tripathi to deal, even before his murder we had sent him but after getting the news of his murder I was very scared that If my name comes, the whole game might spoil... But when I asked for the details of room number 1023, there was no person taking the room as Kailas Tripathi but his name was registered as Alok Purohit. After seeing which I myself was surprised. But believe me, sir, I have nothing to do with his murder." DCP Raghav was not only questioning him repeatedly but also lashed out at Sub Inspector Ashish Sanjay Tiwari. But still the same sentence came out of his mouth It was. But DCP Raghav had seen one more thing in the observation of Sanjay Tiwari so far. On the day Kailas Tripathi was murdered, Sanjay Tiwari was giving a speech at an international conference. His records were already there. Due to this one reason

DCP Raghav had to change his decision. DCP Raghav further says "Until this case is over you will have to stay in jail. Actually, we will decide whether you are involved in their murder or not but your black. "Business is also seen as a crime which has different sections from which you have full right to arrest, so not murder but in other case you need to put in jail we don't need to ask permission from any sector and any commissioner so your hour will be good." When DCP Raghav and Sub Inspector Ashish discuss outside, Ashish asks "Sir you left him like this? He has solid proof of Kailas Tripathi's murder. Not only that, but the report of the foreigner so far and his illegal business, we can say that this person can also commit murder." DCP Raghav says "Ashish we are missing something. We have a lot of characters but something is missing to declare each character 100% criminal. And Sanjay Tiwari is also one of them. The day Kailas Tripathi was murdered one of the Sanjay Tiwari was preparing for the

International Conference from also I used to talk to his debit only and only after coming to Delhi. And the payment was also taken as per hand check so the bank details are also clean. Educated man but misusing. Catching such people can be dangerous further but our main issue is the murder of Kailas Tripathi. Sub Inspector Ashish says "Day by day this case is getting more critical. Every day new faces come. For some time, they show a hope that I am the murderer and soon they have a different story. It starts." DCP Raghav says "That's why we will now look at this case as one where we speak and the other side remains silent." Sub Inspector Ashish asks "So sir I don't understand anything." Once we open the history of room number 1023 there is something in that room that we don't know. It may happen that some clue related to this murder will be found. Next day, when he hears the history of room number 1023, he is also surprised that his head does not work.

Chapter no.9 Some Mysterious Incidents of Room No. 1023

After questioning with the entire people, DCP Raghav and Sub Inspector Ashish decided to visit room number 1023 as well. Exactly what is the history of this room which we do not know till now. Next day DCP Raghav reaches the hotel around ten o'clock, and says to the manager "We want to hear the whole story about room number 1023 where Alok Purohit I mean Mr. Kailas Tripathi was murdered. On that the manager says "Actually sir, for that you are the owner of the hotel Mishra sir's permission has to be taken, because it is strictly forbidden to speak to any staff in this regard. Sub Inspector Ashish "All right, what is the need to take permission for that, we directly ask Mishra sir. DCP reaches Raghav Mishra sir's cabin "Hello Mr. Mishra how are you, hope the identity of the murdered person's real name has reached you. Mishra ji stands up scared and says "Sir really I have nothing to do with that murder." DCP Raghav says “Oh Mishraji why are you so good Whenever I come here, you start your single poem, don't you think that today I have come for some other reason? Mishraji gets scared and says, "Sir, how can I work with the police? Sub-Inspector Ashish says, "Today we want to hear a long history from you, so we have come here with a lot of leisure. Mishraji says "History which history? Sub Inspector Ashish says "It's the same history that the manager is saying is strictly forbidden to tell so we told you to hear it from your own mouth." DCP Raghav says “Room number 1023 Any person refuses to take a room in many times you people also refuse to give that room. But coincidentally, Kailas Tripathi also demanded the same room and when you refused him, you gave him the room in the greed of more money. Right?" Mishraji says "yes sir exactly right". DCP Raghav continues "So now tell me what was the reason behind denying that room and there are some rumors, which we heard some years back. But We did not pay that much attention because it was not our business. But now we have his job so tell the truth or you know we have a lot of method." Mishraji said "Actually sir it was seven years ago. We had a maid Anita who was very beautiful and neat in her work. But then after six months she went to clean that room. And her work was very neat and clean. Even she behaved very politely with every guest, this was going on for many days then one night she got into a fight with some guest and the next day her body was found under the hotel. It was seen in the CCTV footage that she jumped from One Zero Two Three. She was pushed out of room number 1023, some people say she was raped in room number 1023, some people say that the guests staying in one zero two three murdered her and threw her out of that room. This end Because of things and rumors, my hotel suffered a lot of damage, its repetition was decreasing. At that time, the media was silenced by paying money, but now the matter has gone too far. And this is not only after that the room was also locked but after some time, we thought to start registering it once again as it is very comfortable and pleasant for the guest. But why? Complaints always came from that room. Even though the water supply is good throughout the hotel, there is no water in room number 1023, even if fresh food is sent there, it goes stale. While staying at night, his window would often open automatically and some people have also complained that someone would come and knock on the door and when it was opened it would be nobody. So, we have decided to close the number of rooms, but this one night is bringing the hotel into disrepute with such a gruesome murder. DCP Raghav on this Says "Did you get to hear such a good thing about any movie before Ashish?" Ashish laughs at this and says "I don't understand friend why you opened a hotel; you should have become a director, you are making a very beautiful thing..." Mishra says, "Sir, this is the truth, I am not lying. So, I have strictly forbidden the entire staff to speak on this topic. Not only this, we further spoke to Panditji and worshiped that room so that any shadow would leave the room. "But still the whole is the same." "Mishraji what is your education?" asked DCP Raghav. Mishra says, "Sir, post-graduation is done." DCP Raghav laughs and says "Wa wa very well educated and you believe in ghosts and ghosts?" Mishra ji said "That's not the case sir, in fact all these things have happened before. It may be that two things out of five are true but these rumors are the same thing in the head. They are." Mishra ji further says "not only I had a very stressful time but the maid Anita also suffered a severe blow to her father and her father couldn't bear it because of the people raising color on her character and on the same day he also committed suicide." DCP Raghav is very sad after hearing this and adds "well ok what happened in room number 1023 and was his case registered with the police?" Mishra ji says yes sir... but the case didn't last long, ji family Even those who came to stay there that day were not questioned much so the case was soon closed." DCP Raghav says "okay thanks for giving us your time we will see." Sub-inspector Ashish and DCP Raghav then discuss this while going to the police station. DCP Raghav "Ashish what do you think Mishra ji's whole story is 100% true?" Ashish says to her "I can't say for sure. But sir what he told me is my wife. already' said. Because when it was new, my wife was listening to me, so she sent me." DCP Raghav laughs and says "What a story telling lady that I will ever get information." Sub Inspector Ashish says "but sir then your posting was not here, yes this case was very popular but as Mishraji said two out of five things are definitely true." "But sir this has nothing to do with the murder of Kailas Tripathi". Sub Inspector Ashish said. Next DCP Raghav Says "Look, as much as I think, maid Anita should have nothing to do with Kailas Tripathi, but we have to verify this thing. The rest, as Mishraji said, is only correct if we ignore these ghost spirits, otherwise our education will be dishonored somewhere." ' Sub Inspector Ashish says "Well sir then what next?" DCP Raghav says "I want to read Anita's case report once. Only then will we know the secret of this room." The next day was sub-inspector Ashish gives the complete file of Anita's case to DCP Raghav. After reading the case, DCP Raghav realizes that politics has a hand in it. On the night before Anita's death, the Irrigation Minister's son and his wife stayed in room number 1023. So without wasting any time, DCP Raghav and Sub Inspector Ashish arrive to visit the Irrigation Minister's son when they hear an even bigger secret

Chapter 10 DCP Raghav's meeting with Irrigation Minister's son Vinod Chandak

If you look at the reality, the secrets of everything are slowly being revealed in front of the eyes with Mishraji's story. At that time Sub Inspector Ashish says "Sir, please think again, will it be right to meet Minister's son Chandak sir?" DCP Raghav says, "Relax Ashish, it's a casual meeting. I know a little pressure can be created on us, and why should we be so scared to arrest them? "Is running These are just a few things related to the case that we want to know from them." Sub Inspector Ashish says "Excuse me sir, but I am here before you, and I pick that person's character very well, I don't think what story he will be willing to tell us?" On that she is very confident

DCP Raghav says "Don't ask Ashish what his father will answer." When DCP Raghav and Ashish meet Chandak sir, DCP Raghav says "Hello Mr. Chandak, a little with you. I came here because I wanted to inquire." Chandak said, "How did you come here and who gave you permission to come here? First take permission from the commissioner." DCP Raghav threatened, "Let the questioning be done directly, otherwise they will put your name in this case and throw you in." An altercation started between Chandak and DCP Raghav. And angrily slaps DCP Raghav Chandak. Chandak goes completely numb for two minutes. Sub-inspector Ashish looks on in surprise and any policeman gets involved No. Then in a low voice, Chandak says to DCP Raghav, "Sir, what questioning do you want with me?" Then DCP Raghav said, "Isn't it the matter of some people, the minister's son in everything, the sense of ego and all these things are important? If this had been done earlier, there would have been no need for me to work. I don't study in school. We have grown up now. Give the sisters-in-law two teas and you answer my questions." Chandak says "Yes sir." Seeing this picture, Sub Inspector Ashish looks surprised and says in his heart He "corrected the minister's son in one of my god Raghav sirs slapped" Further DCP Raghav asks Chandak "From today seven years in Hotel Kaushalya a maid named Anita took her own life by jumping from room number 1023. And the night before the day she died you and your wife were there and the next Are you telling the incident or what is written in the case?" Chandak says "Actually I was very scared, not only that my father got very angry for this but also She also threatened that she would give many hundreds of properties to my brother. Because it was election time. And because of that, the father also came under pressure, so the father demanded that the case be thrown out." DCP Raghav says "Chandak sir, I am not asking you about your politician background, that is known to the whole world so far how many cases have come up, how many cases have been raffled, but I am not going to keep this case of my life pending. So, I am in that room regarding you. And that I want to hear about what happened in relation to the maid and what was presented in this case." Chandak says nervously "Sir I didn't have any such motto; in fact, the maid Anita was a very good and humble girl. I was literally infatuated the moment I saw her. So I asked her to sleep with me just for one night but she refused and the next day when she When she came to clean the room, I didn't stay. And I caught her forcefully and while doing this My wife saw me, and at that moment my wife and I had a fight and my wife left the room in anger. And we also stopped enjoying ourselves. And sir when I left that room it was only half past nine in the morning." Chandak further says "And sir she died next day between nine in the morning. By that time, we had left the hotel. But due to this Anita's death independent parties attached my name which made our company's party's life even in the election. We had to suffer the consequences. But I really have nothing to do with Anita's death." DCP Raghav gets more confused after hearing this story. Because DCP Raghav felt that 97% out of Chandak Hundred is definitely deteriorating. Because the timing and the exact time he had left the hotel was not related to any of this and somewhere they sensed that he was forcibly dragged into the whole affair. Then DCP Raghav asked only one question “Well Chandak Tell me which Kailash Tripathi do you know?" Then Chandak says "No." Then DCP Raghav and his team leaves from there Chandak's wife brings tea, DCP Raghav says to them "Ok sister thank you come next time let's have tea for sure." Later in the conversation between Sub Inspector Ashish and DCB Raghav, Sub Inspector Ashish says "Sir today I became your fan, a decent person became humble in one slap." Then DCP Raghav laughs and says "We used to be like that Well, leaving it all one thing is certain maid Anita and Kailas Tripathi who were murdered and Irrigation Minister Chandak has nothing to do with these two but still analyze it once. And tell me if you come across any leads." DCP Raghav says "Look Ashish, we have no one to blame now. And even if we are doubting everyone's side is clear, why does my mind wander somewhere as if we are missing some point." Sub Inspector Ashish says "I think sir we should stop listening to people's parable now it’s time to summarize." Yes, I am starting to feel the same way now. Commissioner from above but the pressure is not being handled by me now."

Chapter 11 DCP Raghav got a clue of the subtlety

In the interrogation with Vinod Chandak, DCP Raghav and Sub Inspector Ashish did not get much lead. But when they reached the police station. Then while thinking, suddenly DCP Raghav says to Sub Inspector Ashish "Ashish, we are ignoring one thing." Then Sub Inspector Ashish says "Sir, there is no doubt in Vinod Chandak's statement." Then DCP Raghav says "think carefully, as Vinod Chandak said, he left Sure in the morning, right? "Yes," Ashish said Then room number 1023 must have been visited by some other person after that? On this Sub Inspector Ashish thinks “Yes sir, there is a lot of possibility of this. Immediately afterwards, when visiting the hotel, DCP Raghav told the manager, "I absolutely want the records of your hotel for the past seven years. Manager says "sorry sir we have such old records it is difficult to break give some time. Sub-inspector Ashish says, “Nothing much, we only have that record the day Anita, the maid of this hotel, died. After a few moments the complete records are received and DCP Raghav and Sub Inspector Ashish go through the complete files and CCTV footage from seven years ago. But even here they are seen in confusion. Because the case happened like this, a new couple booked room 1023 almost two hours after Vinod Chandak left the room but their record shows that they canceled within moments. On this, DCP Raghav sub-inspector Ashish Says "Ashish my mind is saying that Kailas Tripathi's murder is somehow connected with Anita's death too. Sub Inspector Ashish says "Yes sir but we don't have the proof we need. Because no record is matching up. And why is the hotel famous for its name, nothing is done properly. After this, the manager says, "Sir, that's not the case, after Chandak left the room, the person who booked and canceled the room got a call from the hotel to cancel it, but he did not. "I don't know that person's name and now how can I find that person in such a large staff?" "Has Chandak come to stay in your hotel before this?" asked sub-inspector Ashish no. To which the manager says "Yes sir came once or twice because mishraji and he had a very good relationship but when the maid and he died then they never even set foot because it was a shock to them and they suffered a lot for that." Sub Inspector Ashish says "Sure Raghav sir."Kailas Tripathi was murdered and what remained was the death of his maid Anita seven years ago was a suicide. So, I think we are looking at this case in the wrong direction." DCP Raghav thinks and says "No no Ashish, we are on the right path, we just don't see the person we want." DCP Raghav further asks "Call the registration staff and members of your hotel." Then the juvenile who was interrogated earlier comes and asks DCP Raghav Kishore

"How many years have you been here teenager?" Kishore says "four years". Then DCP Raghav realizes that Kishore has nothing to do with the incident that happened at the time of Anita's death as the incident happened seven years ago. Then suddenly the manager says "Sir sir a record has been found again. After canceling the room on the day Anita died seven years ago, there is a booking again as Prabhat Kulkarni." Then DCB Raag ordered to extract the details of Prabhat Kulkarni immediately. But There were not many details in the record, Prabhat Kulkarni's photo was not clear enough so it was not only difficult to understand, his phone was also attached but it was coming up as not reachable. And of course, the record from seven years ago should be satisfied now when even the police were not very keen to find out where the person is now. DCP Raghav was acting very annoyed and came out in a rage. And in this situation of theirs To add to the beauty of the program, the commission sir also got a call, who after talking to them was acting even more annoyed. The then Inspector Ashish explains to him "Sorry sir I salute your dedication but one thing is not convincing but still I want to tell you.... Actually, seven years back that case was very much in the limelight no person was always refused to stay in that room. Because many people have claimed to have a soul there." DCP Raghav is exasperated Ashish gets angry and says "Ashish I didn't expect this from you. You also believe these things to be true. Really you should be ashamed. Such things are giving rise to superstition. A small thing is making a big rumor. Our job is to bring justice to the criminal for which we have to do it." Such superstitions should not be believed." Later DCP Raghav feels remorse and says to Ashish "I'm sorry I didn't want to say that to you". Then Sub Inspector Ashish says “its Ok sir no problem."

Rather than spending time on who Prabhat Kulkarni is like, we should do a proper verification of the direct aspect that is in front of us. Because now is not the time to trust anyone and listen to their story." To which her inspector Ashish says "Yes sir, for me you should take some rest today, you are not feeling well." Then DCP Raghav says yes Ashish I am taking some rest tomorrow come to the office with complete details then we will discuss.do."

Chapter 12 Adverse effect of the case on DCP Raghav

In fact, there were so many questions, sub-inspector Ashish and DCP Raghav reached the spot without losing their deputation to seek answers to each question. But his work was not getting the desired success. Only a new direction was being obtained so that DCP Raghav could not sleep while he was resting. Because Kailas Tripathi's murder in room number 1023, and Anita's seven-year-old suicide in that room, greatly affected his mind and head. Was But he was a senior officer, so even if his mind was affected, he was not one to give up. But they needed some time to get out of it all so that it would focus properly. After some time, Sub Inspector Ashish comes there and says "Sir don't give up like this please we get courage seeing you and if you act like this then how can we get courage?" Raghav then says, "When no way opens, he has to force it."And without him there will be no way forward." So far what we have done or not done in this case is not important but what we will do now? Forget how many people were involved in the case in your past and start keeping an eye on the people who are newly involved." Everyone starts getting courage automatically. Then a list of the new people who joined the case was made and they started right by adding their minute movements related to the case. It was looked at, their call records, their past history, their identity, their work, education, etc. And all this he got a small success which was called "Prabhat Kulkarni". A small piece of information from Prabhat Kulkarni served to completely turn the case for him. Prabhat Kulkarni found an important reason for staying in room number 1023 seven years ago... and this There was a reason for which Professor Sanjay Tiwari was arrested. "Drugs and Mafia Supply". After getting this lead, Sub Inspector Ashish immediately informed DCP Raghav. Then DCP Raghav says "Ashish now we are going to hear the last parable related to this case and now after the story is over only our fines will work." They take out Sanjay Tiwari who is in the crowd and put a single proposal before him. "Look professor sir now we are all fed up so don't make any story about what it really is Tell us otherwise we have been given complete freedom by Commissioner sir." Sanjay Tiwari knew that now no one will save him from here and taking any person's name is a threat to his family so he told the same things that he knew. "Sir actually I also don't know how any person is involved in this drug supply but we only and only supply drugs by misrepresenting our identity in the hotel where we stay so that any scam Even though these things mislead the police, on that day also one of our team members booked a room as

Prabhat Kulkarni and showed a fake certificate, but on that day, he got a call to cancel the deal as there was a suicide case in the hotel as Anita. And then on the third day of the suicide case, he left the room." DCP Raghav "What is the real identity of Prabhat Kulkarni tell me soon and don't examine my patient otherwise you are the one who murdered Kailas Tripathi in this case. I will close the hair by making hair on you." "Sir his real identity is Kailas Tripathi whom we used to supply under a different name." Sanjay Tiwari said this in a panic. After that Sanjay Tiwari got a lot of police work and he was put in jail and new cases were framed against him under hundreds of IPC sections. Somewhere DCP Raghav was satisfied as he found another person involved in the case It also helped a lot in solving two or three cases. But still there was one regret in their mind that is why did Anita commit suicide? And what was the compulsion with Alok Purohit aka Kailas Tripathi, a brilliant person who got the status of a scientist and a professor, who got into this evil business? Then Sub Inspector Ashish comes there and says "I am happy that we got a success but sir with success in everything we don't get the success we want. One more thing sir I feel like this. So, I think the hotel staff and its owner are also involved in this case." DCP Raghav says "I have this suspicion too. But which persons shall we involve in this case?" Immediately after that they go to the hotel and ask Mishraji "Now you must have seen the news on TV how Sanjay Tiwari confessed his crime and he had to go to jail in new new cases." On this Mishraji says, "Sir, we have helped as much as we can, but it is a scholar There were no professors and also to stay in this room for a large amount of money, so we kept dealing only and only, we did not know anything about their business. And many people say that Anita's suicide was the girl's fault. All three that Prabhat Kulkarni attracted whoever it was and had physical relations with them in such a way that it was a lie in her character that's why she committed suicide, so don't put that case in your mind." "Mishraji you are so much I am doing my work, but if you don't have the proper identity of the person staying in your hotel and what kind of business they are doing, what are their exploits, if you keep quiet, then remember Sanjay Tiwari next. The news will be yours," DCP Raghav threatened.

Chapter 13 – This lesson of superstition surprised DCP Raghav!!

In fact, DCP Raghav did not believe in any such things as souls, ghosts, corpses, he was against the fact that such things as souls and ghosts exit this world. But this was the moment in his life that he would get to hear all these things every day. Later, when he was working on a case to investigate the front, he got a new acquaintance with this lesson. the whole Investigation of the case was going on at the spot. All the employees in the hotel staff used to have a different look and fear from DCP Raghav. If he asked any question, he would answer it truthfully. Because there was one thing in everyone's mind, that if DCP hides anything from Raghav, he will take that thing from us with great trouble. When DCP Raghav inquired with the people, 95% of the people used to hear negative things about maid Anita. Like that character There was no girl, proud of her beauty, she used to subjugate men and have immoral relations with them, and sleeping with every person for the night was nothing new to her. But when DCP Raghav's mind takes a closer look at things, he keeps one of his goodness in his head. But no one thought that the murder case in room number 1023 would be related to Anita's suicide seven years earlier. All files, all Details, repeated viewings brought new things and new things were solved but the killer of Kailas Tripathi was still at large. Just then they get a call from Kritika from Forensic "Raghav sir, Prabhat Kulkarni who came to live in that room seven years ago is Kailas Tripathi, it is 100% true because Kailas Pati's blood sample matches with his report, we just checked in the old records." Over time, the case lost interest in the media as well This is because the media covers only and only the latest. The Commissioner's interest in the case was also slowly waning as Kailas Tripathi's family was also not concerned, so they did not take action. Slowly the people's attention was drawn to the new things, the hotel was also trying to run smoothly but the curiosity of one person i.e., DCP Raghav to hear the secret of the murder in that room number 1023 and to find him was not gone yet. Something though After a month, the order to look into new cases came from the Commissioner Sir. He decided to focus his attention on it. And then one day after a few months, they went to the hotel for tea. After sitting outside the hotel, the hotel guard came beside them and sat down. That guard says to DCP sir "What are you saying sir how are you?" DCP Raghav smiles and says, "Okay uncle, what are you saying, how are you? Have you started a new job here?" "How many years have I been here? That’s it, baby," said the guard. "Oh, sir but last time when the case was going on here, I came here many times and you never saw me" said DCP Raghav. Then the guard says "Who has the leisure to look at a poor person like us sir. Well leave these things, did that Anita get justice. I had a little faith in you, that you will give justice to that child" DCP Raghav regretting it says "what can I say uncle there are some things which are in the hands of the law and not in me. Begged a lot that I want to solve this case completely. But the case was closed even I could not give justice to those who killed Kailas Tripathi so gruesomely." Then the guard said, "Sir, don't feel bad. That man's karma was bad, that's why the dog died. There was nothing wrong with that poor Anita, sir. She was a very hardworking girl from a poor family and lived with her father. That night, she was attacked. Kailas Tripathi tried to force her upwards He raped her and also blackmailed her by recording a video, in which the poor woman lost her own life. In such a situation, that Kailas Tripathi wanted to die." DCP Raghav, who was listening curiously, was totally puzzled and thought to himself, "I have never seen this man in this hotel before, but how does he know all these things?" Then DCP Raghav says to the guard "Can you say with hundred percent certainty that her suicide case is not suicide but murder?" Then the guard Crying he says "Yes sir I have many proofs too but I never presented it to anyone because only and only politicians live here, any suicide case is suppressed and a poor person like us does not get justice." "Well tell me your number and your name now I will go to the police station and report this to the commissioner sir or you come to the police station with complete evidence and now we will see who will stop this case." said DCP Raghav. Then the guard says "I have a phone No sir, my name is Ramu Tote. And works as a security guard here." DCP Raghav calls the police station in a hurry "Hello Ashish come to the hotel early, room number 1023 has met a really big lead." Ashish comes to the hotel with the entire police force. Next DCP Raghav and entire police personnel go to the hotel and there the entire staff, manager and hotel owner Mishraji also come, everyone asks "Sir, suddenly what work is left in this hotel?" "Anita who committed suicide in room number 1023was done and also we will get solid evidence about the person who killed Kailas Tripathi," DCP Raghav said. Everyone is surprised and then Mishraji asks "Sir but who is going to give you proof?" Mishraji the guard in your hotel is going to give me all kinds of evidence he knows everything about this case but never saw him in all these days. Mishraji orders "Call Sharmaji" then DCP Raghav says "Oh wait wait, call ramu Kaka, Ramu Tote, call him. Not sharmaji" Then everyone gets surprised and says in their hearts that DCP's mental condition is corrupted, this man is going crazy, he has a big impact on his head, some doctor has to show him. Mishra ji also puts his hand on his head and says to Sub Inspector Ashish sir I beg you "take DCP sir to some good doctor he is in dire need and please stop bothering us." Sub Inspector

Ashish also Agrees to things and takes Raghav out. DCP Raghav doesn't know why everyone is behaving like this with him and why everyone is looking at him with surprise? Or Sub Inspector Ashish says to DCP Raghav "Sir you really need to take leave I'm sorry I shouldn't say this but you are really affected." Then DCP Raghav asks "I don't know what you are talking about Ashish. And why are everyone looking so surprised?" Then SB Inspector Ashish says "Sir the Ramu Tote you are talking about is Anita's father, who hanged himself within a few episodes of Anita's death because he could not bear that his daughters committed suicide. Because he could not bear the bad reputation of the girl." So, they lost their own lives. Now tell me what evidence can a person who is not in this world give you?" Hearing this, DCP Raghav immediately goes away and is declared a leave for one installment So that it is well prepared by focusing on your health. Yet again and again the same thought came to their mind, then who was the guard who spoke to me? What spirit was that? Are ghosts really corpses? She still couldn't believe these things but till the end the murder in room number 1023 is still unsolved.

Chapter 14 Summary of this novel of room number 1023

After some time, the entire case was

completely closed. Many stories of this were spread in the media but it lasted for a few days and after a few days it also stopped. One thing is clear from this whole thing that there are thousands of cases which are still pending, a small ray falls on them and it seems that now it will be opened like for example Sushant Singh Rajput, big suicide cases of big people, there are many more cases whose Who was behind, who wasn't, who is.etc But one lesson we can learn from this whole novel is that we should never make fun of any person's feelings. Because we never know, tomorrow that situation may also happen to us. It is a mystery that

Kailas Tripathi was murdered in room number 1023? Who was the person who promised to give complete evidence related to the case to DCP Raghav? Was it really and his father? Is Anita's spirit still in the room that murdered Kailas Tripathi? Did you take it? All these questions are yet to be answered. And not only this, many such things happen in the world but due to the media and some rumors it is shown through a little wrong way so that superstitions are sometimes promoted to a large extent. But if the present generation needs, we should try to teach them well so that everything is logically correct. Not only this, another surprising thing is that in that room any the person was not seen coming and going, was the murderer present? And exactly seven years later, when the same person came to stay in the same hotel room, how come he was murdered? Not only this but further Kritika who was in forensics also told DCP Raghav over the phone that the time of death of Anita and Kailas Tripathi was exactly the same at 8:27 AM. But the government needs evidence, we cannot solve the case without feeling anything. and if there is any secret, it is not necessary for the world to know about it. Because even the government cannot give justice to some things, in such a situation, if any person gets justice by going against the government, then it is not wrong. So, it's not really wrong. And in this regard, how big is the crime of rape and whoever did the rape criminal is a criminal. If he is escaping from the clutches, it would be right that he is murdered instead of escaping. So, let's meet in one such new novel based on true events

- Author Shreyas Ghadge.

CPSIA information can be obtained
at www.ICGtesting.com
Printed in the USA
LVHW041942220323
742311LV00004B/228

9 789357 334372